"In a world where manufacturing and technology are such an integral part of our live Andrea has shared the secret to embracing chang through agile practices in No Disruptions. By focusin on the middle market Midwest, this book uses rea world applicability to manufacturers located an serving a perceptive market. Delivered by honing th Midwest as the focal point, Andrea has provide readers nationwide the enigma of transforming th snares we watch so many manufacturers fall victim to to join the lean concepts and practices vital t remaining one-step ahead of the competition. Andre has skillfully identified and illustrated the processe needed to accept change and take advantage of th opportunity it holds. Having read hundreds of book few deliver precise and immediately applicab solutions such as No Disruptions. Andrea's wisdom h been generously and exquisitely weaved througho these pages."

Dr. Jennifer Beam
Founder & Executive Consult
Association for Leadership Practition

No Disruptions

The New Future for Mid-Market Manufacturing

Andrea Belk Olson
CEO, Prag'madik

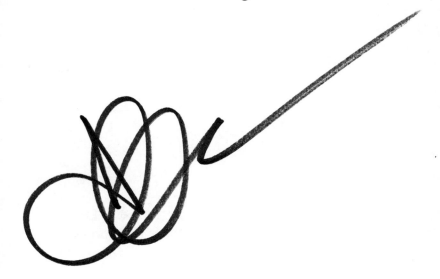

www.nodisruptions.com

Edited by Colonel (Retired) Burl Randolph, Jr.,
MyWingman, LLC
Cover Design by Andrea Belk Olson
Foreword by James Claassen

Contact the Author
Andrea Olson, Founder/CEO of Prag'madik
Email: andrea.olson@pragmadik.com
Website: www.pragmadik.com
Twitter: @pragmadik

ISBN-13: 978-1530913671
ISBN-10: 1530913675

For my father, Darwin.
A manufacturer and perpetual craftsman.

TABLE OF CONTENTS

FOREWORD

This book is for and about middle-market US manufacturers in the Midwest, but more importantly, across America. These thousands of companies work to supply major OEM's such as John Deere, Alcoa, Caterpillar, Boeing, and countless other multi-billion dollar corporations. These manufacturers are well suited to provide their products at competitive rates, with healthy profit margins for the long haul, *or are they?*

As a technology and marketing veteran, Andrea Olson has taken her extensive experiences working in the manufacturing industry, to outline the pitfalls and potential for the small and mid-sized manufacturers that support many of these more prominent OEMs. "No Disruptions" will no doubt cause discussion within the manufacturing industry in the heartland, which is good. Family owned or controlled businesses need an impetus to change, or our national OEMs will begin to outsource many of the services that have kept the region vital for so long.

Times are always changing, yet in this digital age, it is even more important to be agile and responsive to change. There's an honor and nobility with doing things the old fashioned way, but not at the expense of the long-term health of your company and its employees. Many small manufacturers have survived hard times, pulling things up by the bootstraps to face the toughest challenges: building a real business with sweat equity. But sweat equity only goes so far in the new, digital age. It's about working smarter than your competitors, continuous improvement, and staying ahead by embracing change. Change, the great constant, variable, and disruptor of the universe, can be costly, intimidating, and frankly, downright scary!

Yet only a rolling stone gathers no moss.

James Claassen, CEO *(Retired)*
KONE Elevators & Escalators USA

INTRODUCTION

Most people cringe at the thought of change, but there is another event even more disturbing than change: Disruptions. At home, work, school, even at the gym, disruptions are constant and the bane of Drucker's (2004) Effective Executive. How are we expected to accomplish anything with constant disruptions? The Constant Disruption mentality has turned one industry on its head: Manufacturing. Controlling disruptions to production lines is so critical to manufacturers of all shapes and sizes; there is what I call the Manufacturers Mantra:

NO DISRUPTIONS

With the stage set, what are disruptions but the precursors to change? Unfortunately, manufacturing has taken No Disruptions to such an arcane level that the mantra threatens the very existence of the manufacturing industry in the United States. No Disruptions is a cautionary analysis of the threats to the small and mid-sized manufacturers within the US, if significant disruptions or changes do not occur soon. "Made in America" is a slogan as old as the country, and the resurgence of the popular catchphrase has created a manufacturing mania of sorts. This mania however, has yet to address the four biggest detractors of No Disruptions: emerging technologies, the global market place, the speed of information, and the generation gap. With everything to lose but also everything to gain, the manufacturing industry needs to embrace disruptions as the means for the small and mid-sized US manufacturers to remain viable, and make "Innovation in America" the manufacturers new mantra.

If you are a business owner or C-level executive, consider the legacy you leave for your company for the next generation. We all know that the balance sheet, profit and loss (P&L) and cash flow statements guides a small company's month-to-month operations, but it's not only your financials that count – it's also your processes, infrastructure, employees and market position. Although you might have a patented product that costs you little to produce, it doesn't mean you're handing over a stellar company to a successor. Whether it's about pride, money, or legacy, use the opportunity today to leave behind a company that is better than you found it.

Companies that have not continued to advance business processes and infrastructure will be extinct in the next 5-7 years (Sheth, 2015). Larger companies will internalize production or seek modern suppliers overseas. "Cheap" no longer means value. If it costs a company more time and effort to do business with you than to pay a higher price per piece, they will make the fiscally intelligent decision and select a better business partner. The mounting pressure to control operating costs requires a paradigm shift within entrenched, old process manufacturers, where orders are faxed and sales are tracked via terminal screen. We need a paradigm shift that forces owners and executives who dismiss technology and marketing as an "added cost", to see both as operational benefits and the path to securing larger customers and contracts.

Even the federal government has continued to modernize its online bidding and contract award system. In 2014, the Defense Information Systems Agency (DISA) began changing the face of federal procurement with a new federal program called the Integrated Defense Enterprise Acquisition System or IDEAS. IDEAS is a natively mobile, cloud-based, shared services solution designed to meet the contract writing and acquisition needs of the entire Department of Defense (DoD). O'Connell (2014) wrote that IDEAS is capable of delivering acquisition management that supports each DoD agencies unique procurement needs without requiring costly manual workarounds. IDEAS operates at a fraction of the traditional operating and maintenance costs associated with similar systems, which traditionally require desktop installs and in-house IT maintenance teams to monitor performance, hosting and customization. IDEAS is a whole new way of conducting business. Automation within this 'acquisition-as-a-service' approach allows digital applications to be much more streamlined, which improves time-to-business value and employee efficiencies.

With these types of systems coming on line, it becomes more and more important to have the technical capacity to connect to these systems, digitally and dynamically. This will require the right employees to help implement, sustain, and effectively promote the right systems. It is an impending inevitability, which in due course will separate those companies that embrace and survive the digital age, and those that die like the dinosaurs of yesterday: faxes, brick phones, and compact disks to name a few. You can "bide your time" and "keep your head in the sand", or embrace change, because it's coming regardless.

CHAPTER ONE
The State of Disruption

It is easy to get the impression that American manufacturing has entered a new period of revival. Many in the media, along with consulting firms and economists, now tout the term 'manufacturing resurgence' (McCutcheon, 2012). Pointing to companies that have re-shored production back from overseas citing rising costs abroad, and reduced costs at home, these optimists assert that the U.S. manufacturing sector is both resuscitated after its decline in the late 1990's to early 2000's and repositioned to accelerate in the coming years.

If only that were completely true. According to Nager and Atkins (2015), U.S. government data paints a different picture, where American manufacturing has failed to recover back to 2007 output or employment levels. In addition, the lion's share of growth appears driven by cyclical rather than structural recovery, and as such, may represent only a temporary trend.

After a decade of unprecedented decline in U.S. manufacturing from 2000-2010, the industry, the public, and policymakers are rightly eager for any sign of good news. Since its peak in 1979, U.S. manufacturing employment has declined, with moderate losses through the late 1990s, mostly caused by increased manufacturing productivity relative to the rest of the economy. Since 2001 however, with the rise of China and the new globalization, U.S. manufacturing employment experienced a decade of unprecedented losses, shedding 5.8 million jobs, or about one-third of the workforce (Nager & Atkinson, 2015). The manufacturing job void equates to over 17,000 manufacturing establishments lost since 2013, a staggering amount.

But unlike the prior two decades, those losses were caused not by superior manufacturing productivity growth, but rather by significant losses in real value added output, from product differentiation to the customer engagement experience. This in turn caused a large increase in the U.S. trade deficit (Nager &

Atkinson, 2015). By 2002, a deficit in advanced technology industries also surfaced.

Low-paying, low-skilled jobs that Americans do not want were offshored to nations such as China that compete only on cost. Offshoring then freed up the American economy to focus on business services and advanced technology products where its comparative advantage truly lies. Manufacturing employment losses could be explained by low-cost production abroad, productivity gains decreasing the need for labor, and a natural shift away from manufacturing toward a knowledge-based service economy. Although reporting on manufacturing seems dismal, there is a light at the end of the tunnel.

The Opportunity of Disruption. Through a disruption within the industry, U.S. manufacturers have a great amount of opportunity in creating new value for customers. These new opportunities may come in the form of new products, industries, or applications, but even more significant, how suppliers interact with customers. Front-of-the-house operations (accounting, customer service, sales, marketing, engineering, project management, and purchasing) have been consistently far behind the streamlining or leaning-out of shop floor and manufacturing operations.

While manufacturing processes have continually but gradually modernized, business operations have lagged woefully behind. The slow adoption of new technologies, software, operations automation, and resistance to employee training, has all contributed to the hindrance of value-added operations growth. The separations between antiquated business practices and modern manufacturing processes, especially within small and mid-market manufacturers, have caused a chasm within those organizations. The results are stifled growth, stagnated sales, and in some cases, closed doors.

With tightening budgets caused by a continued slowing economy, companies have looked at numerous measures just to maintain current operations. These measures include cutting costs in high-dollar areas, examining procurement, switching suppliers, eliminating overhead, and increasing sales staff. More draconian methods include the dreaded Three R Strategy of restructuring, reducing, or retiring products and services. Sometimes entire product-lines and departments were eliminated

(Cameron, 1994). Some companies have started to look externally for support, identifying potential mergers as a solution, acquisitions to stay in the market place, or pursuing buyers for the company. Although cost-cutting measures are important and necessary, many manufacturers have begun cutting too deep, and eliminating value-added areas that differentiate their business. The inability to differentiate between creating efficiencies and producing effectiveness has resulted in companies boiling down their businesses to simply providing products or supplies.

Creating a Disruption. Inevitably, short-term tactics reduce long-term strategies to nothing more than price competition, and suppliers who were previously unique, are now commodities. A paradigm shift in manufacturing mindsets and strategies must occur both at a local and national level to change this trend. This paradigm shift will create a disruption requiring a comprehensive overhaul of manufacturing's image. The 'trickle down' impact will also create the need to overhaul manufacturing strategies, executives and employee's behaviors, and a dramatic transformation to keep business competitive.

The optimistic view is that there is ample room for change, in turn creating opportunities for growth. The pessimistic view is that all changes cause disruptions, and to keep production operations steady and on time, there can be no disruptions. Mid-market manufacturing is an integral component of the U.S. economy, and its decline and eventual consolidation to a handful of players will impact everyone. With mega-manufacturers as the new normal, small, privately owned shops may go the way of the cassette player: Useful in its day, but overcome by the technology of MP3s, iTunes, and music streaming services. Technology has its time, and the time is now as we work with a tech-savvy and intensive generation.

CHAPTER TWO
The Reality of Working with Our Kids

I was halfway through my first pint when he said, "I'd never consider a job in manufacturing. I'd rather work at McDonald's." The young millennial, who we will refer to as 'Tom', intended to finish his Bachelor of Science (B.S.) in Engineering in a few months and, had been pouring through job postings, attending career fairs, and imagining where his lofty career would begin.

I vividly remembered the feelings of optimism I had when I graduated. It felt like I was truly starting my "real" life. I was in control of my own destiny, ready to tackle the world. Overzealous, overconfident, and overwhelmed by the looming burden of that adult problem called student debt - nothing and no one could stop me. I believed in myself and the vision for my future.

Tom lamented, "Manufacturing doesn't offer...well, the same opportunities as other industries, like IT or healthcare". "It's a dead end." *Manufacturing, a dead end?* What was he saying? Now a seasoned professional, I had spent half my career within manufacturing, working for two different global organizations. They afforded me the opportunity to travel internationally, expand my professional experience, and learn about everything from FIFO (First In, First Out) to ISO (International

Organization for Standardization). How is that a dead end?

Observing my confusion, Tom tried to justify his statement with, "It's hard to explain..." he muttered, almost seeming embarrassed. "I have a few friends that got jobs at manufacturing companies. It's not that they don't get to use what they learned in college, but...it's like...going back in time." Now glad we had a chance to speak, I knew this would require further sustenance to continue the conversation, so I raised my hand to flag the bartender as I'd exhausted my pint. Finally, I asked, "What do you mean by that?"

Continuing on, Tom said, "Well, my one friend, Mike, works at a privately-owned company. There are only about 200 people there, so he thought it would be a good opportunity to have a lot of responsibility, without a lot of corporate bureaucracy." Tom took a drink and cleared his throat. "But there were so many issues. First of all, their data infrastructure was terrible - using a so-called Enterprise Resource Planning (ERP) system that was little more than a database, without the ability to extract or analyze information. Large files couldn't be emailed, and had to be physically delivered to different locations on a flash drive."

I could see Tom's demeanor relax a bit as he continued to explain. "Even worse, Mike became a minor casualty to the unwritten 'status quo' rule. Anyone that had suggestions or ideas to improve processes faced the wrath and resistance not only from coworkers, but also from the ET - Executive Team. On one occasion, a C-level leader told Mike directly, 'If it's not broke, don't fix it. We don't try to reinvent the wheel around here.'" Tom's comments gave me pause. I had heard and seen this type of environment before, but it had to be the exception, not the rule. There are hundreds if not thousands of major manufacturers that are much more ahead of the curve. "What about your other friend?" I asked. He couldn't have had the same situation, could he?"

Tom answered, "No, James worked for a huge, global company. He had access to the latest design software, worked with a large team, and had great benefits and pay. His problem? He felt stuck in a silo. Assigned to a very narrow scope of work, focused on doing the same thing day-in and day-out, without opportunities for new projects or upward mobility, he was a cog in a wheel. James equated the experience to being on the manufacturing floor punching out widgets."

Dismayed, I took a slow swig of my beer, thinking for a moment, careful to chose my words. "Well, the Silo's of Excellence mentality is a challenge in any industry. It's hard to stand out in a large company, and small companies often have financial restraints that limit fast change and growth.

I would not disparage the entire manufacturing industry for only two unhappy instances, – when maybe neither Mike or James had the right fit." Tom sat still and looked thoughtfully. Finally he replied, "Agreed. No job or employer is perfect. It's the fact that manufactures seem to be in a bubble. It's like they don't realize the world around them is changing, or maybe they just don't care."

I paid the tab and shook Tom's hand. As he grabbed his coat and cell phone, I said "Thanks for chatting, I appreciate your thoughts and opinions."

"No problem." Tom said, "Don't get me wrong; I know I have to start at the bottom, but starting in the dark is unacceptable". "I refuse to start at a company that's operationally 10 years behind." I stared into my empty glass, wondering about how many newer grads were thinking the same thing. There is a new cliché, but the meaning is timeless:

"The struggle is real" (DTMD, 2011).

The struggle to attract one generation of workers into the industries and vocations that helped their parents pay for their educations, and put roofs over their heads, is all too real. Struggle often creates fear, and fear is a powerful force that transcends generations.

CHAPTER THREE
The Fear of Lean

"Just set up a Kaizen event to address the problem."

When *The Toyota Way* was introduced in 2004 (Liker, 2004), it made a huge impact on the manufacturing industry in the United States. The Toyota Way caused a revolution in lean production - and tons of other publications promptly followed. Focused on the highest cost center, The Toyota Way addressed how to streamline operations. Key

19

principles centered on productivity, reducing waste, standardizing tasks and developing people, all helping move forward operations mired in excess time, activities, inconsistency and risk. Thousands have written case studies detailing the progress made throughout organizations, including Just-In-Time (JIT) manufacturing and Kaizen.

Consulting companies sprung out of the woodwork, creating classes, courses, training seminars and programs to teach organizations these Lean Six Sigma-based processes. While manufacturing streamlined, the front-of-the-house never received the same treatment or attention. Companies that have adopted The Toyota Way often had an internal leader who spearheaded the effort. A Chief Operating Officer (COO) or equivalent had both the power and influence to propose this type of transformation, and the capacity to lead the organization through the effort.

Other organizational departments were not so lucky. Fragmented by structure and function, business operations have continued to lag behind this level of modernization. Many new processes, platforms and software were developed in the past decade, but were only adopted piecemeal, such as a new accounting system or cloud-based design software. The biggest challenge to implementing *The Toyota Way* is synchronizing it across the entire organization. Although designed for manufacturing, the Toyota management philosophies can be reduced to four core principles that apply to business operations: Taking the Long-Term View; Having the Right Processes; Developing People; and Continuous Improvement.

Principle #1 – "Taking a Long-Term View"

Taking the long-term view centers on sustainability, and how your business processes can scale efficiently. If you had to cut your "white collar" workforce in half tomorrow, could you accomplish the same organizational objectives? How much information and "tribal knowledge" exists amongst only a handful of people? What if you had to dramatically up-scale overnight? Would you have the infrastructure and intellectual capacity to handle it?

It seems easy to add more customer service, accounting or marketing personnel, but each of these skillsets is added overhead. Furthermore, people are expensive and have a finite capacity. Taking the long-term view means examining how your business operations can survive and function in both the best and worst case scenarios. These scenarios require not only having the right people, but also the right processes.

Principle #2 – "Having the Right Processes"

Having the right processes focuses on identifying the right problem, and matching it to the right solution. The influx of software "solutions", including ERPs, MRPs, CRMs, CMSs, (Enterprise Resource Planning; Material Requirements Planning; Customer Relationship Management; Content Management System) and a whole host of other acronyms, claim to be the silver bullet to all business processes. These platforms can solve a plethora of challenges, but the harder questions are: Which challenges need addressing, and when? This brings us to Raymond Loewy.

You might not have heard of Raymond Loewy. You might not know that he had a brief career as a fashion illustrator. Even further, you may be unaware of his unmatched revolutionary impact on industrial design. In 1949, TIME magazine deemed Loewy the "Father of Industrial Design" (Campbell-Dollaghan, K., 2013; TIME, 1949).

Loewy worked for more than 200 companies as a consultant, creating product designs and logos for the likes of Shell, Greyhound, Exxon, the U.S. Postal Service, Frigidaire, Studebaker, NASA, Coca-Cola and many more, well known corporations. His approach and outlook, though hailing from the 1930's and 1940's, remains valid today. More specifically, Loewy lived by what he called "The MAYA Principle".

What is The MAYA Principle? In short, MAYA means "Most Advanced Yet Acceptable". Loewy believed that the public was not necessarily ready to accept logical solutions to their problems/requirements, if the solution implied too vast a departure from the norm (Dam, 2016). MAYA is a very important principle not only in design, but also in change creation and management within an organization.

The trend in 2016 is to center around "disruptive technologies" and concepts, bringing to market something that challenges the status quo. Although this may be all-well-and-good, it is not as easy inside organizations where processes and procedures are entrenched within legacy systems that serve as the infrastructure for the entire company. How you approach implementing a change - including the size, breadth, and timing of the change - all impact your success. Loewy inadvertently developed the principle of the buy-in: Winning the hearts and minds of people, regardless if you are right or wrong. Even though many improved manufacturing processes abound, everything ultimately revolves around people.

Principle #3 – "Developing People"

Developing people targets your highest cost center: human resource management. While manufacturing and assembly processes require skilled and non-skilled labor, many business operations can be automated for low to moderate cost. The value of the knowledge, problem solving skills, experience and unique talents that cannot be trained are what help propel an organization forward. Duke and Udono (2012) wrote that people are the most precious asset in an organization, and cannot be easily replicated or replaced. I would take a few liberties in believing that Drucker (1967/2006) – The Father of Modern Management, would agree that spending money on people to push paper or implement task-heavy processes, is a complete waste of time, talent, and treasure, in an environment that increasingly requires knowledge versus manual workers.

The critical elements to employee retention are to ensure they feel valued, and are continually challenged to grow. If the majority of their time is spent on non-value added activities, you have a recipe for losing over-achievers and holding on to underperformers. At the end of the day, if you are not advancing and improving your operations, your people will remain just as stagnant. If you allow your systems to deteriorate over time, that then becomes the new system, and the new obstruction to changing organizational culture and improvement.

Principle #4 – "Continuous Improvement"

Continuous Improvement focuses on eliminating complacency. How many processes have been done the same way for years, if not decades in your company? Lack of change can be just as deadly as too much change too fast. Just as organizations justify investments for new equipment to reduce time and waste, the operations and systems in the front-of-the-house (accounting, sales, purchasing, marketing, customer service, human resources) should be assessed the same way. From simple software upgrades to platform integration, these systems should be part of your continuous improvement efforts, whether through incremental steps or breakthrough innovations.

The common stopgap to organizational growth is adding personnel, which typically is the first resource reduced once the organization hits a downturn (Davis, 2004). What is your cost for recruiting and onboarding new employees? Between the time and effort to recruit, integrate, (process their paperwork, set up their profiles on your network) train (get them up to full productivity, and conduct an initial evaluation of capabilities), a single entry-level employee can cost you over three times their base pay rate in one year (Taylor, 2016). Continuous improvement as a routine business practice is designed to avoid the high costs of employee attrition. The fear of continuous improvement, a philosophy that has been in the marketplace for decades, is just another impediment to the forward progress the manufacturing industry needs to make. When proven methods of productivity improvement are not readily accepted, what happens when new innovations in manufacturing occur? New innovations are seen once again as old obstacles.

CHAPTER FOUR
The Fear of Change - The Innovation Gap

"We don't need flashy technology."

Innovation is the new buzzword injected into the global conversation about manufacturing. Advanced technologies, robotics, and automation, are now part of the manufacturing landscape. The heart of economic growth in the Midwest is manufacturing, and innovation must play a key role. Through agriculture, steel, foundries, and a wide array of other specialized manufacturers, markets have flourished, cities have expanded, and economic development has grown in double-digit percentages (Nanney et al., 2014). Manufacturing, to the Midwest economy, is like technology and entertainment is to the West Coast. Because of technology and innovation, long gone are the days of being covered in black soot, shoveling material into a kiln, and over time developing black lung or some other wretched disease. *Or are those days really gone?*

Large, global manufacturers, including companies like John Deere, Caterpillar, and Alcoa are the gold-standard models for the future of manufacturing (Rakowski, 2003). This level of manufacturing excellence occurred through modernizing all of their business practices and processes. Embracing digital technologies to streamline communications, data management, and overall business operations improved operational efficiencies and managerial effectiveness. Suppliers to the large manufacturers - often mid-sized, privately owned commodity manufacturers - can be years, if not decades behind the times in terms of technology. The challenge of change with these suppliers most often manifests in one of two forms – internal cultural resistance and the lack of understanding of how to effectively implement technology within the business. Yet, the bottom line in either scenario is fear and resistance to change, which stifles forward progress.

There is an observation in business called Moore's Law (Thackray, 2015) stating that the capacity of a transistor doubles every 18-24 months, and will continue to do so for the foreseeable future. In laymen terms, this means the rate of today's technological change is compounded, and for each year you fall behind, the gap doubles.

In a national survey to mid-sized manufacturing suppliers, a Nanney, Michaels, Goverman, & Rosone (2014) Deloitte survey found that mid-market companies' view of technology is becoming increasingly enthusiastic. Of the respondents, 41 percent reported their leadership views technology as a "critical differentiator and key to growth," while another 38 percent view it as "a strategic investment." Fewer organizations now view technology as simply "necessary" or foundational, and as a result, more companies are using technology as a means to increase the top and bottom lines. Technology is no longer seen as a pariah, but is now used to meet the needs of both the workforce and the customer.

The Nanney et al. (2014) survey also revealed that many companies are embracing change and expressing a healthy appetite for innovation. Thirty-six percent of respondents dedicated at least 50 percent of their Information Technology (IT) budgets to implementation of new technology versus maintenance of existing systems. The sentiment is even more pronounced among private equity-owned firms. Among this subset of companies, 45 percent of executives responded that they direct at least half of their IT spending toward investment in innovation. Nanney et al. (2014) indicated this suggested a considerable degree of confidence in the potential of new technologies among investors backing these firms. Technology has now become a strategic imperative for growth.

While it is an exciting time for mid-market companies as they adopt new technologies, the environment is not without challenges. Almost 25 percent of respondents in the Nanney et al. (2014) survey reported that it is difficult to keep up with the rapid pace of change in the technology landscape. Others seemed overwhelmed by the prospect of diving into the data their organizations produce, and questioned whether they will be able to analyze and take advantage of meaningful insights.

At least 27 percent of respondents cited the challenges of dealing with unstructured versus structured data as the biggest hurdle in using analytics. Additionally, approximately 33 percent of respondents expressed continuing concerns about the security of the data, and the services provided by cloud-based solutions. Nanney et al. (2014) also highlighted some behaviors that illustrated additional challenges and potential causes for concern. Twenty-five percent of respondents reported information security has had the most significant technological impact on their organizations over the last 12 months. About 40 percent of respondents also believed that they have not taken adequate steps to ensure their companies are prepared for cyber-attacks. Cyber-security exposures can cause irreparable harm to companies of any size.

Through the National Center for the Middle Market (NCMM), Boyer and Moutray (2013) also conducted a study, and found that Advanced Manufacturing Techniques (AMT) have the potential to significantly improve production output and profitability for manufacturers, ultimately serving as a catalyst for economic growth. Boyer and Moutray further discovered that the technologies most frequently used by middle market manufacturing firms—which represents 17 percent of U.S. middle market revenues, and approximately 33,000 companies—primarily included automation, computer technologies, process technologies and information technologies. AMT consists of a family of activities that (a) depend on the use and coordination of information, automation, computation, software, sensing, and networking, and/or (b) make use of cutting edge materials and emerging capabilities.

The survey findings indicated 78 percent of non-AMT users stated that they expect to implement advanced manufacturing techniques over the next three to five years. Key motivators for adoption included improving profitability and strengthening margins.

Currently, 47 percent of middle market manufacturing firms indicated current advanced manufacturing use. Those firms were mostly in the upper end of the middle market revenue spectrum, at $100MM - $1B, were more likely to maintain some international presence, and maintain established expansion plans. Users of advanced manufacturing nearly unanimously stated that the techniques have had a positive impact on profitability. On average, those firms reported a 20 percent increase in profitability over the past five years, a net increase in jobs over the past year of 3.4 percent, and an anticipated further 4.7 percent growth over the next 12 months.

Regardless of the AMT used, approximately half of those surveyed reported a skills gap, particularly in the area of technology. More than 57 percent of AMT users found a need to routinely re-train their workforces to utilize new technologies, while 42 percent reported that special technological skills are now required of new hires. The cost savings for the production line may be consumed in training and re-training costs.

The manufacturing landscape has changed, will continue changing, and with it, the demands on organizational skillsets and culture to embrace it. Embracing technology is only the first step in cultivating a culture of innovation. Gaining an understanding of how technology can transform front-of-the-house operations, processes, and customer insights, enable an organization to compete more effectively, invest smarter, and grow more efficiently. Using AMT effectively requires insight on areas of the business where processes can and need to change.

Coupled with AMT processes are establishing what we call advanced people techniques or APT. APT requires developing the necessary skillsets needed to implement and sustain new processes. Companies have great internal resources, and with some training, will rise to the occasion. In other cases, the gaps are clear but unfortunately, will demand being addressed through recruiting new hires. There will also be experienced employees and leaders who are resistant to change and counter-productive to a new outlook – that have to be let go. An examination of your entire team, from the executive team to the shop floor, is required to fully understand where your gaps and opportunities lie. AMT is a massive undertaking, but if you haven't cleaned house in decades, it is long overdue. Although a massive undertaking, AMT is merely a precursor of the change to come.

CHAPTER FIVE
Impending Disruptors

"Our customers have always bought from us based on our relationships - they will never buy our products online."

With the advances in digital technology, customers' expectations of service, responsiveness, and performance has dramatically changed. Traditional communications via fax and mail, taking the course of days and weeks, has changed to instant updates from a phone app. When 2025 rolls around, traditional supply chain models will be extinct, according to the 100-plus thought leaders and partners behind the U.S. Roadmap for Material Handling & Logistics. The report identified different disruptors prompting transformational change (Prest, 2015). These disruptors carry over outside of the supply chain, into the business operations, strategy and long-term competitiveness.

While often viewed as a challenge for the retail and consumer industry, this expectation of performance has begun to carry over into other industries, including logistics and manufacturing. People run businesses, and once the bar of performance has shifted in their daily lives, it's only a matter of time before that expectation migrates to the workplace. For example, less than 10 years ago, a phone call would have to be made to find out the status of an order. Today, one can simply go online and see where the product is in production, along with projected shipping and delivery dates.

BMW has perfected this digital transparency. When a new BMW is ordered, an individual owner can track the entire process online, from initial order specs, production stages, transport status, pre-delivery preparation and final delivery to the dealership, all by simply having the VIN number (Boeriu, 2009).

This transparency of process engagement is essential to the future of mid-market manufacturers. With increased pressures from OEMs and suppliers, visibility of process and delivery, along with responsiveness to issues, questions and concerns, are soon becoming the new baseline standard.

The impending disruption of digital technology carries with it the obligation to modernize not only infrastructure, but also people and processes. Just some of the disruptors that are here and on the horizon include:

E-commerce: Online purchases will be a full 10 percent of all sales transactions by 2017 (Prest, 2015). This is because of both increasing use of mobile devices and transparency/access to information through digital mediums. Enabling online purchasing also provides a platform for more intelligent sales and customer service, including automating wear part reorders and transparency to purchasing patterns.

Mobile and wearable technology: Nearly 60 percent of Americans owning and using a smart phone to shop and track purchases (Prest, 2015). The embedded global positioning system (GPS) capability in these devices can also be leveraged to enhance deliveries. This technology provides visibility to in-field product location, along with opportunities to actively track product performance for warranty insights and quality improvements.

Robotics and automation: Autonomous control, driverless vehicles, and wearable computing—integrating these into production and operations systems will produce for revolutionary change in the industry by removing the potential for human error and performing tedious or dangerous tasks humans don't want to do. Automation can be used to enhance product differentiation by eliminating high-risk maintenance and service activities, within your internal operations and external service calls.

Sensors and the Internet of Things: The proliferation of embedded sensors that communicate in real-time via the Internet without human intervention supports the Internet of Things. Among the opportunities: sensors in manufacturing could warn of problems and offer instructions for corrective action. This information can then be leveraged to impact future generations of product design, including increasing safety while lowering on-site service time and costs.

Big Data: Managing and leveraging the massive amounts of information companies collect and store about operations, sales, and customers requires advanced computing power to analyze and visualize the data. Organizations no longer have to look back to reconstruct what happened; they can apply sophisticated algorithms that perform predictive analytics to anticipate and prepare for future scenarios, thereby mitigating risk. Big Data is not about the quantity of information, but capturing and leveraging the right information to answer critical business questions to become more competitive and efficient.

Workforce: Manufacturing has an image problem. Although many facilities of the past no longer resemble those of today, as baby boomers retire, the industry is challenged to attract, train, and keep an adequate workforce. The industry must find new ways to appeal to a very different workforce: women, veterans, people under the age of 35, and differently-abled persons. By marketing, branding and positioning your company as modern and forward thinking, it will be easier to attract a workforce with that same mindset.

Sustainability: Societal pressure for corporate responsibility dictates that the industry must address the environmental impact of manufacturing operations in order to mitigate its effect on local wildlife, solid waste generation, and polluting emissions. Sustainability isn't simply centered on being a good citizen – it can also be a profit center, enabling the generation of new sources of revenue through identifying new ways to reduce and leverage waste.

Collaboration: Existing technologies can significantly reduce the inherent cost associated with manufacturing by leveraging the data held by suppliers, manufacturers and OEMs. To truly reap the benefits, however, these companies will have to establish trust in order to collaborate. With transparency to information, including inventory and lead times, suppliers and OEMs can more accurately manage resources, eliminating the all-too-frequent "fire drill" when orders dramatically increase or decline.

Manufacturers must prepare to meet the challenges of the next decade, by embracing and understanding disruptors – viewing them as opportunities versus costs. Simply investing in infrastructure, technology or human resources is not enough. Organizations must formulate a strategic plan that includes core competencies and future business objectives, and is in step with customer expectations and the changing, competitive marketplace, in order to survive.

CHAPTER SIX
Millennials and Manufacturing - An Issue of Image

"Our work is hands-on, hard and dirty."

Think of the old photo where there's a group of ironworkers sitting on an I-beam at the top of the Empire State Building in New York City, eating lunch. While the advent of unions, safety regulations and worker rights have all but eliminated these types of scenes; there is still a strong component of hands-on work. From a skilled tradesman to an assembly line worker, hands-on work retains a special meaning to the true craftsman lost on the technologist.

An Issue of Image. The manufacturing industry continues to promote the profession with visuals of individual welders wearing a helmet laden with an American flag, while piecing together large metal objects. Other impressions include a series of female workers in hard hats observing an assembly line, and a minority worker wearing safety goggles and applying a sticker to a finished product.

While those are all critical and value-added positions to any manufacturing organization, none of those images convey *personal growth*. The ads often show roles that are often times limited in upward mobility, and delivers only incremental pay increases over many years. In addition, these images positions manufacturing solely as a *hands-on* industry, leaving behind key functions such as engineering, marketing, accounting, human resources, procurement and logistics. Many up-and-comers from business schools to trade schools need to fully understand that manufacturing companies can provide long-term career opportunities, but manufacturers need to communicate those opportunities.

An Issue of Opportunities. The lack of perceived opportunity amplifies the current skills gap that exists in the manufacturing market. Skilled talent shortages shift power to the employees, enabling them to seamlessly move from organization to organization, based on who has the best upward mobility prospects. The next generation workforce is seeking growth, whether that is skillsets, education, or both. A LinkedIn (2014) study discovered that 85 percent of the workforce is actively looking for a job or open to talking to recruiters about better opportunities; even those that are *satisfied* with their current job. This exodus is fueled not only by the standard "better compensation and benefits packages", but also by the number one driver: Greater opportunities for advancement.

In the traditional sense, promotion always denoted advancement. Today's workforce has a new definition of advancement, with a stronger emphasis on work/life balance. In a knowledge-driven economy, employees seek to grow their personal and professional lives simultaneously. This has redefined "advancement" to mean learning transferrable skills, expanding areas of responsibility, and immersion in new technologies. Although there are many major global manufacturers who can provide those opportunities, smaller suppliers continue to struggle to meet the demands. Even with an offer for higher wages, smaller manufacturers often have outdated equipment, processes, and infrastructure, creating limitations that are a huge challenge when it comes to acquiring top talent.

An Issue of Appearance. When a candidate enters a facility run by outdated software, old machinery and paper-driven processes, it compounds the stereotype of manufacturing being "behind the times". With an issue of appearance, potential employees see little to no path of adding value to their own knowledge and skillsets, and see an organization resistant to modernization and change. Many manufactures turn to human resources to support recruitment, pushing for better and more skilled candidates. Unfortunately, without the same investment in business operations that occurred on the production line, human resources departments in smaller organizations lack the skillsets and staff to effectively "sell" the company to potential employees. The content and images used to promote the organization are often overused and non-differentiating, recycling overhead shots of dirty shop floors, boring warehouses, or individuals at outdated terminal screens, conveying little to no excitement, challenge or growth. On the issue of appearance, a picture truly is worth a thousand words.

All manufacturers face the ongoing challenge of finding and securing skilled persons for the shop floor. While there are many theories in place as to why the next generation of employees is not seeking skilled trade jobs, the challenge is partially born from the industry's history itself. Throughout the 1990's and early 2000's, Generation X and Millennials, saw their parents in manufacturing positions lose their jobs to a combination of outsourcing and automation. Smaller shops quickly closed, with their assets purchased by larger companies, where wages continually decreased. In the end, the manufacturing industry created an unspoken reputation as a dead end, undervalued, commodity business.

Why would anyone want to enter an unstable market, where you could lose your job overnight? Why would you want to take a risk going to a small shop that could quickly be overtaken by a larger competitor who replaces the current workforce? Employees want stability, and to have stability requires increasing your own personal value to an employer. Value in an ever-changing world cannot increase in an organization with antiquated processes and technology skills. A change needs to occur throughout small to mid-sized manufacturers.

This change requires taking a hard look at how to reposition the manufacturing industry in the eyes of potential employees. More importantly, looking at change through the eyes of potential large customers, who are requiring suppliers to be more agile and technology-savvy. This shift has to take the form of progress on multiple fronts – communications, human resources, marketing, front-of-house processes, and digital infrastructure. Because the battle for new talent is intense, and mediocre talent will seek a job, but great talent will seek a career with long-term opportunities. For manufacturers to thrive and prosper, attracting and retaining this new talent is critical to the survival of the organization. Baby boomers are in the midst of retiring, and knowledge, skills and experience must be transferred to a new generation of workers, to continue propelling the manufacturing industry forward.

The battle for new talent is not simply the hiring and training of a new wave of employees; it's about a transformation of culture. Lorsch & McTague (2016) published the results of a cultural reform survey in the Harvard Business Review. The survey involved current and former CEOs who had successfully led organizational transformations. The CEOs unilaterally agreed that culture is not simply something you "fix", rather it is what you get after you have established new processes and structures to tackle tough business challenges. The culture evolves as that work is implemented, and the team rises above the challenges presented by the external environment. One such challenge is how to incorporate new technology, both in your front-end and back-end operations. Although new technology may be an opportunity for growth, to 'lifers' in an old organization, it may be seen as a threat.

CHAPTER SEVEN
The Fear of Technology

"But we've always done it that way."

Manufacturing prides itself on process - a level of stability and consistency that drives production. Essential to profitability, this stability is inherently "anti-disruption". In the recent past, disruption concerns usually stemmed from the supply chain, production, assembly, and even logistics. Today's disruption risks spring from lack of data access and transparency, just-in-time production demands and overall operating cost reduction. These risks are larger and more looming than they seem, and cannot be addressed as simply and cleanly as procuring a new raw materials provider.

With the advent of ERP systems in the late 1990's, automation became all the rage, yet, as soon as this new technology started to be embraced by industry-leading organizations, the first-wave fallout ensued. Horror stories of SAP implementations gone wrong plagued the manufacturing world, with operations coming to a complete halt for weeks or months at a time as the common theme. Ill equipped to understand or effectively implement such wide-sweeping systems; companies relied on vendors to lead the effort. Vendors, however, often did not fully understand the manufacturing process. Many of the systems at the time lacked the ability to handle and effectively manage custom jobs, attempting to shoehorn in a non-standard process into a formalized structure. ERP systems and SAP implementation left many companies reeling from the fallout.

The Foundation for Fear. Feeling bruised, battered, and burned from the fallout and failure of new systems, companies often reverted back to old tried-and-true systems. The vow to 'never again waste money on massive technology investments, becomes the new culture for the organization. This attitude created a chasm between those organizations that successfully made the technology leap, and those that continued embracing legacy platforms. Companies that adopted new technologies continued to grow and advance, learning from experience, and were more capable to assess and evaluate their needs. Adaptive Manufacturers (AM) became more acclimated to

65

technology and their resistance to change diminished. As software and platforms continued to advance, those organizations continually upgraded systems and processes, expanding IT departments to support growth and transition. AM were able to leverage their experience in new ways to reduce operating costs and gain insights on customers and suppliers to be more competitive.

Legacy Manufacturers (LM) are those that made the conscious decision to ignore new technology, and have continued to dig a proverbial 'deeper hole'. Fear became the new friend of the organization, as old systems and processes were now fully entrenched, and the cost and risk of moving to new technologies seemed overwhelming at best; and company killing at worst. Immediate returns from those investments were hard to define or justify, as older systems became more and more costly to unwind from day-to-day processes. The hidden costs of holding onto antiquated systems and processes are larger than you might think. According to Baran (2012), including people and technology, it takes approximately 4.4 days and costs $4.60 to process a single invoice for a best-in-class operation. The least efficient organizations can take up to 34.4 days at a cost of $55.00 to process a single invoice. We refer to this as a 'leak-in-the-bucket' – non-value added costs to your business that reduces your overall profitability.

A Fundamental Law. Applying the 'leak-in-the-bucket' concept across the myriad of transactions and data that flows through an organization daily, the net loss of non-value added operations could quickly reach into the tens of thousands. Although it is likely cost-ineffective to analyze each and every element of your business, it may be reasonable to estimate as a rule of thumb, that each step in an inefficient information management process (such as order processing) costs $5 (Driscoll, 2011). Multiply that $5 transaction costs across each step, multiple transactions, and multiple individuals, and it quickly adds up over time. Even if you consider this a low estimate, this $5 'sunk' expense costs organizations an inordinate amount of money. Cutting this by even 50 percent could deliver a solid ROI on the majority of digital investments.

In *The Toyota Way*, Liker (2004) laid the main foundations of Lean Manufacturing, and described the Seven Wastes existing in Manufacturing: transportation, inventory, waiting, defects, over-processing, excessive motion, and over-production. To identify areas in a process where improvement is needed, the Seven Wastes need to be identified and then measured. While most of these wastes are visible and easily quantifiable in a manufacturing environment, they are more difficult to distinguish and measure in an office environment. Nonetheless, these areas and their associated costs need to be addressed to effectively compete in the future.

The Secrets Hiding in Data. We should also consider the risk of sunk costs for data extraction processes, which keep floating to the top. Even though information may seem simple to maintain in your current operations, it is essential to examine the scale of expertise in that system, both inside and outside your company. If only one or two people effectively know how to extract data and maintain that information, you in essence have a single point of failure. If that individual chooses to leave your company, your operations may essentially come to a grinding halt. Does this single point of failure risk permeate across multiple departments? Digital improvements transcends outside of manufacturing and accounting operations. Logistics, marketing, sales, shipping, and customer service all have a role when it comes to utilizing operational data. Other areas of your organization may be hamstrung with lack of access to dynamic data, especially if this access is solely sourced through an individual or the IT department.

Single points of failure and silo's of excellence also limit operational efficiencies and proactive problem identification. Departments using "canned" reports often have a predefined view of data, and limited transparency to what additional data is available. This view degrades determining new ways to generate revenue, eliminate waste, and capitalize on opportunities. Digital upgrades are about three things: processes, information, and analysis, requiring all three to gain a measurable benefit. Cliché's abound in American culture, and 'you only know what you know' is a popular one. If a business only operates with the same information, in the same way, with the same processes, for decades, identifying new questions to ask, or to effectively identify where future challenges lie are nearly impossible. The fear of technology occurs in both our personal and professional lives, but one tool – marketing communications – is what successful businesses use to help us overcome our fears.

CHAPTER EIGHT
Why Marketing Matters

"We don't need marketing. It doesn't work."

Marketing is a polarizing subject. Some organizations will swear by its value, while others define marketing by the tactics used: tradeshows, brochures, websites, etc. Manufacturing has limited utility for embracing marketing. Often perceived as an unavoidable cost, marketing is often undervalued

73

and underutilized. Sales are the king of cash flow and yet in manufacturing, effective marketing may be the difference between flat sales and accelerated growth.

Every department in your organization has both a strategic and a tactical function. In lieu of cutting costs, manufacturers have reduced their marketing departments to solely an implementation team, primarily outputting brochures and maintaining the company website. With little to show for the effort in the form of direct Return on Investment (ROI), marketing budgets are continually reduced year-after-year. Long term, this continued reduction in marketing pushes organizations further behind in both market presence and market image. In short, *if you fall off your potential customer's radar, it's a long and expensive process to get back on it.* There are four core strategies to leverage your marketing investments beyond tactics, into areas of the business to impact market share, differentiation, and risk.

Marketing Leverage #1: Market to increase market share

Many manufacturers believe that organizations make purchases on facts. Technical specs, price, and availability – they all come into play, yet people drive every organization. When comparing similar products, potential customers need a compelling argument and understanding of why what you produce is better and different. Generic terms such as "quality" and "industry-leading" have become overused and all but meaningless. Your sales team knows how to tell a compelling story to individual prospects – the tactical fight. Your marketing needs to take your story to the masses - the strategic fight.

Marketing is the primary mechanism for building awareness and increasing exposure to the market for your product. It gets the phone to ring and gives your sales force new customers to meet with. While many companies use marketing as the "make it pretty" function of the organization, they need to be leveraging it as the "make us compelling" function. Simply put:

Marketing preps the prospects for the sales force.

Stereotypical tactical marketing activities such as email campaigns and Facebook updates, lack strategic impact. When devising a marketing program, you must first focus on strategy. Marketing strategy should align with the organizations strategy, vision, and mission. After alignment, the marketing strategy starts with identifying the problems you are trying to solve, and the markets you desire to influence. The mechanisms, timing, and approach should be designed around those problems, through the lens of your target audience. With the continued reduction in marketing resources and skill-sets within industrial organizations, the opportunity to leverage this area of the business as a strategic asset remains unrealized, and will eventually become a lost art.

In the commodity business, differentiation is critical. Manufacturing organizations often attempt to compete on the two typical fronts: quality or price. Price, in the long term, can be a losing battle, with raw material and overhead cost fluctuations. Quality can often command a higher sale price and margin, but today's quality buyers are demanding more than just an end product alone. Marketing is integral to bridging the gap between positioning an offering as a commodity versus a value-added solution to a customer's operation. The more effectively an organization can tell and support that story, the stronger and quicker market share is gained.

Marketing Leverage #2: Market to differentiate and streamline operations

Marketing is about communication, positioning, and perceptions. People and systems control communication - how information is shared within and outside of an organization. Legacy-based organizations center their internal and external communications on email, Word documents, and Excel spreadsheets. While these tools create a simple process it also creates extremely time-intensive and high-risk, in the highly vulnerable digital age. By continuing to rely on legacy systems, information can be lost, overwritten, or easily sent to a competitor by mistake.

More importantly for a customer or vendor, what is the *cost* of doing business with your organization? What are the *benefits* of doing business with your organization beyond your products and services? Differentiation can, and should, go beyond deliverables, to a level where the cost of doing business is simple, streamlined, and transparent. Platform integration with customer's purchasing systems, automated invoicing, and inventory transparency, can all eliminate non-value added hours to both you, your customers, and your vendors. Taking systems a step further, scheduling and automating online reordering of wear parts can eliminate both a potential lost sale for a company, and ensure a customer always has the parts on hand when they need it.

Although most organizations would charge IT with these types of efforts, there is a unique difference between the process of specifying a software platform and the features and functions it has to serve. Marketing should bring to the table the insights of how people use information, and spearhead how these internal and external communication systems are designed, centered on usability and differentiation. If your marketing department is not involved in all areas of communication throughout your organization, you essentially have an internal documentation department.

Marketing Leverage #3: Market to reduce business risk

If 80 percent of your business is done with one customer, there's a high risk of that customer jumping ship, even with receiving the best price and quality. While many manufacturers have long-standing contracts with key customers, this lack of diversity makes an organization beholden to one source of cash flow. Organizational stability stems from a diverse customer base, and marketing should be the driving force to build this diversity.

Organizations may see building diversity as the sales force's job, to hunt down new prospects and convert them to paying customers. While often this is the result of sales tactics, the actions prior to the first meeting are what truly set up your sales force for success. First and foremost, new prospects need to be aware of your company and have a clear understanding of what you deliver. Even though your sales team is pounding the pavement, there's virtually hundreds of thousands of potential customers worldwide that you can't effectively meet face-to-face. Marketing should help drive and shape your image in the market, so when they do pick up the phone or visit a prospect, half the battle is already won.

Reputation is synonymous with brand, and your brand is shaped by actions. There are however, many actions and differentiators that set companies apart, which are never articulated to the market or capitalized on. Manufacturers continually miss the opportunity to effectively tell their story to prospective customers by centering communications solely on quantitative figures. Without qualitative information, or the narrative story to support the figures, manufacturers don't effectively *sell* their products and services.

The uphill climb to gain new customers then becomes steeper and costlier, and most organizations return their focus back to serving and maintaining an existing customer base. Over a period of years, as customers are bought, sold, and acquired, your revenue mix is reduced to a handful of channels, where even the loss of one customer can be devastating. If your marketing efforts are not building that portfolio, they are not serving the long-term needs of the organization.

Marketing can be a strategic asset to manufacturing, if it is effectively understood how marketing adds value, and how to capitalize on that value. Marketing is partially a sales function, but more importantly it is a business function. Marketing has the ability to transform operations, beyond just external promotions and prospecting. Forward-thinking manufacturers must learn to embrace and empower their marketing teams to push beyond tactical implementation, to build effective marketing strategies. Marketing creates for businesses, the avenue to break away from the status quo.

CHAPTER NINE
Status Quo Culture

"If it's not broke, don't fix it."

Manufacturing industries in the United States have a long-standing history. Built from the ground-up, many of the mid-market companies now have second or even third generation owners. Learning the trade from their fathers before them, today's owners face a daunting challenge – breaking out of their comfort zones. When companies have been passed down through generations, often there is a process-learning gap. Being embedded so tightly within a company can shield individuals from seeing and acting on bigger picture changes within the industry. It is very clean and simple to identify needed upgrades to machinery, facilities or new ways to eliminate high scrap rates. The challenge is identifying where technology and new processes can reduce costs, increase productivity, and differentiate.

Sadly, many mid-market manufacturers have a solid team of "lifers" – those employees that have been with the organization for decades, and have lived through the ups and downs of change. They know their job, they know your systems, and have a familiarity that enables them to help on-board new employees, which increases their perceived value to the organization. The lifers are often the same individuals that are the 'resisters' to change, and solidly embrace the status quo culture.

The Lifer Legacy. Lifers are extremely valuable to organizations, however, have limited exposure and experience outside of the company. Lifers often cling to "existing ways of doing business", and justify those perceptions through input from key customers who are also mired in their own status quo. The underlying issue is that they miss the big picture – the changes within the overarching industry that demand reducing paper processing costs, overhead, and streamlining business unit operations. Without an external perspective, whether from a consultant or a new employee, family owned or controlled businesses will continue to resist change, chalking it up to high-costs, the challenges of customer education or simply the fact that their system "isn't broken".

Maybe the current system is not broken, but older operating systems have many downsides. For manufacturers, their legacy infrastructure limits:

- The ability to properly scale. This often requires software to be installed and maintained on individual machines rather than a cloud-based platform accessible from anywhere, anytime. This "legacy system management" can consume on average 60 to 80 percent of IT department budgets (Driscoll, 2011).

- Older platforms are often no longer maintained by the original developers to develop patches, fix bugs or upgrade security flaws, making data within them at risk of loss or theft.

- Have limited security roles, where there is no transparency to who accesses information and when.

- Are not friendly to integration with other systems, requiring manual work-a-rounds, including exporting data into Word or Excel, and manually entering back into another system.

- Have limited or no data analysis capability, requiring manual creation of business reports by exporting and cross-comparing data, with high risk of errors.

- Limited or no availability to add new features or customization without a high up-front development cost from a third-party.

The question is not if a system is broken, but rather if your platforms and processes are restricting growth. In Carroll's (1865) Alice in Wonderland, there is a theory referred to as the Red Queen Running (RQR). RQR suggests companies must run – not walk - to continuously keep up with the fast moving landscape. There are many middle-market firms squarely in the race, yet there are many challenges and barriers in their paths, which slow them down.

The Advantage of AMTS. A NCMM study found that 47 percent of middle market companies note that they use Advanced Manufacturing Technologies and Systems (AMT), but even more important, they report an average profit increase of 20 percent based on these technologies. In numerous research studies (Boyer & Moutray, 2013), being proactive with manufacturing technology has been shown to be a critical strategy for success.

The average increase in profits of 20 percent however, obscures the reality that there is great variability in results. Research in numerous studies has indicated that companies should spend more on training - perhaps twice as much - than on buying the actual technology. Boyer and Moutray (2013) also found that users of these new systems allocate 8.8 weeks on training – substantially more than non-users. This is of critical importance since there is a positive relationship between training, performance, and adoption.

Businesses must maintain flexibility, both in terms of what technologies to invest in, and how they are applied. It is critical to carefully consider what technologies are the best fits, and allocate investments accordingly. Much research has shown that careful investment strategies are critical, and interestingly, the mix of technologies is relatively constant over the years. The highest ranked AMT today are automation and computer technologies, and process infrastructure systems, such as ERPs and CRMs. Just as important as flexibility in which technologies to use, is the need to remember to use them to make the organization more flexible. Research has consistently shown that using technology to be agile is a better strategy than simply using technology to increase output and replace people.

Although the Boyer and Moutray (2013) study showed that middle-market firms most value AMT to improve production and efficiencies to increase profitability, the research suggested a cautionary note. Simply increasing production efficiencies alone is not a sure route to increased profits for manufacturers. Just as important is the ability to increase the output of what the customer wants. Creating flexibility to meet customer desires also helps increase profitability, and reinforces change management.

When faced with changing the status quo culture, manufacturers should remember the adage that patience is a virtue. Advanced Manufacturing Technologies often have a long lead-time between implementation and increased performance – often several years. Fifty-seven percent of companies have to regularly re-train their workforce to keep them abreast of advancements (Boyer & Moutray, 2013). The path to progress is an ongoing transformation. Much like self-improvement, the job is never done, because the environment and challenges change constantly.

CHAPTER TEN
Risks vs. Costs

"We don't need to add unnecessary costs."

Innovation can be a word associated with both risk and cost. In the 1980's, the introduction of Microsoft Office revolutionized virtually all businesses, and even manufacturers went from traditional carbon-copy paper processes to a digital data platform. This shift was partially a forced adoption, because suppliers and customers demanded information in a non-print format. The second wave of revolution came in the 1990's with the advent of ERP systems, where entire operations moved to a digital space, automating everything from inventory to production process management.

Many mid-sized companies failed to make this second leap, often times because of the massive organizational shift and the large up-front investment required. Those organizations continued to maintain outdated platforms throughout the subsequent decades, adding-on tertiary automation systems, without integration into the core operating system. The result: An unwieldy mix of different systems for different operations of the business, requiring a high level of hands-on information management by personnel.

In the 21st century, the software landscape has dramatically changed. With the introduction of cloud computing and software-as-a-service (SaaS), the steep costs of platform integration have been significantly reduced. Additionally, the usability of these systems are continually optimized and improved, coupled with extensive training and support programs. The pains of technology integration in the past are not what they used to be.

For manufacturing companies, the potential benefits of cloud computing and SaaS are becoming increasingly apparent. Technology functions handled off-site in the cloud can free up internal IT teams for more productive tasks. A virtual network can save both physical server space and reduce capital costs. An integrated suite of sales, manufacturing, and accounting applications in the cloud can "speak" to each other and streamline handoffs of information between individuals and departments, reducing miscommunication.

Mid-sized industrial companies are expressing greater confidence in cloud computing and operational software technologies, because it helps meet their business goals. Consider the proliferation of the resources in the cloud. A manufacturer now can manage a range of employee benefits by tapping into SaaS, enabling an HR department to meet specific talent management needs through cloud-based tools. Likewise, cloud computing can enable mid-sized firms to satisfy customer technology requirements without the responsibilities of ownership.

Much like the fixed costs of owning a car, a data center requires facilities, hardware, and engineers. Cloud and SaaS solutions basically enable a company to "lease" a solution, rather than shoulder the burden of complete ownership. SaaS technologies can also enable business-critical staff such as installers, to be trained off-site or on-location using cloud-based project planning systems. This type of flexibility saves costs, but also transforms the customer experience, improving responsiveness and automating follow-ups to increase the effectiveness of closing a sale.

According to a Giffi et al (2015) survey, at least 50 percent of respondents reported that many functions - especially finance and accounting - are already cloud-based or are in the process of shifting to the cloud. In fact, reluctance to try cloud computing has all but faded. Only 2 percent of B2B (business-to-business) companies said they are waiting to adopt cloud-computing solutions, a tremendous reduction from 14 percent two years ago. Also, over the past two years the percentage of B2B companies reporting "mature" deployments within cloud computing increased from 9 to 21 percent.

Lineage Logistics, a warehousing and logistics company that provides cold chain solutions to leading food, retail, agriculture and distribution companies, recently migrated to the cloud to help consolidate a range of front-office functions, including finance, invoicing, and payroll. Chief Information Officer Sudarsan Thattai said the breadth of the company's cloud adoption was prompted by its acquisitive nature: Lineage was founded through the combination of premier regional temperature-controlled warehousing companies, acquiring 5 of its 18 legacy companies over the last year (Nanney et al., 2014).

Integrating newly acquired companies' IT systems in the cloud is now much easier — taking as little as 90 days — and Lineage eliminated its "stranded islands of investment" (legacy software platforms and in-house maintained systems) by significantly reducing its owned IT infrastructure. "We were spending an inefficient amount of time and money integrating our acquisitions into the Lineage infrastructure," said Thattai (Nanney, 2015), who added that his dedicated staff of four was able to manage the cloud migration in less than 14 months. "With a cloud solution, we are able to focus on what really matters — delivering innovative, sophisticated and customizable supply chain solutions to our customers."

Despite such examples, cloud computing and system modernization has not taken over exclusively as the go-to technology model for the middle industrial market. Rather, the picture is more complicated. Most industrial executives have challenges with identifying and determining the platforms they need, and struggle more with an effective implementation and rollout. These organizations also often lack the internal resources to support such a complex effort.

Tradition also plays a role. Many organizations have IT departments that are built around legacy systems that represent substantial investments and individual job security, due to "tribal knowledge". Making the switch to new systems incurs complications and costs, which may suppress some companies' appetites for switching. Even with these barriers, this traditional view continues to hamstring the opportunity for industrial companies to break out of old business methodologies and effectively compete in today's agile market.

CHAPTER ELEVEN
The Youth Market

"Those Millennials don't have the right work ethic."

The younger employees of today, Millennials, do not live in the past. Having grown up with technology, Millennials have a very different perspective and expectations on how communications and businesses should operate. Those of the Baby Boomer generation had to take the extra effort to capture information. Think back to the days of the card catalog in the library, perusing microfilm of old newspaper clippings, or drudging through what seemed like a 1,000-pound reference manual.

The Millennial generation, born with Google, has always had the ability to instantly access information. Additionally, this generation of workers has the experience of "immediate and intelligent response" from companies. Think about your customer experiences from digital companies like Amazon, Zappos and Apple. Intelligent product recommendations, automated customer service, and proactive communications all play into the new level of expectations of today's consumers. The industrial sector deserves no less.

Hands-on work has retained a level of romanticism that is often unappreciated. Having to wade through the details to solve problems the hard way can be seen as reflecting a strong work ethic. Yet, with today's technology, Millennials are continuing to ask the question of "Why work harder, when you can work smarter?" It is an important question, and one worth asking in a different manner: is your team spending time on activities that are adding value to your business, or is it just busywork?

With the huge influx of technology companies into the marketplace, not selling products or holding inventory is a very lucrative proposition. The ability to use software to become agile has enabled tech savvy companies to pivot their focus almost overnight. In the manufacturing space, this flexibility is not so easy. With customer demands of having in-stock inventory and holding raw materials, all for the ability to customize solutions, creates a heavy overhead to bear. Inventory overhead has to be managed and maintained with a steady sales and cash flow, without the luxury of changing the business model on a dime. The demand from the next generation of employees however, will require manufacturers to re-examine how they do business, and be open to new disruptive approaches and technologies in the marketplace.

Consider, for example, your supply chain. Many raw materials at competitive prices can be sourced as far away as China. Holding enough production inventory for a calendar year requires accurate sales projections, controlled waste, and a proactively timed order from the supplier because of long lead times. While this supplier might be the most cost-effective, a Millennial might pose the questions:

- Are there local suppliers we can set up to have a back-up system, and supply us at a lower cost?
- Can we discuss deals with local suppliers to hold inventory as needed?

- Can we automate reordering when supplies hit a "low quantity" threshold, eliminating the risk of someone forgetting to reorder?
- Can we use technology to set up a bid system to provide all potential suppliers the opportunity to do business with us, without making hundreds of calls and follow ups?

As you can see, the opportunity to go beyond the basics of choosing and evaluating suppliers, to using technology to have suppliers compete for your business changes the game. It puts manufacturers in the drivers seat. This simple scenario exemplifies how the younger workforce can influence the way manufacturing organizations can modernize their businesses.

The Millennial generation also demands challenge, growth and security. These individuals saw their parents work decades in one company, only to see their position downsized or shipped overseas. They are inherently suspect, and justifiably so. The Millennial generation understands that to get ahead, you must continue to grow your skills, to add value to yourself, which in turn, adds value to an organization. If you're doing the same thing day-in and day-out, on an antiquated system, with highly manual processes, those are not portable or differentiated skills. Most often, they are only unique skills to that company. In addition, if that organization is not continuing to advance their business processes and practices how long will they continue to *even be* in business?

According to Giffi et al. (2015), over the next decade, the US will require nearly three and a half million workers for manufacturing jobs, with the "skills gap" accounting for nearly 2 million of those jobs going unfilled. There are two major contributing factors to the widening "skills gap": Baby boomer retirements and economic expansion.

An estimated 2.7 million jobs are likely to be needed as a result of retirements of the existing workforce while 700,000 jobs are likely to be created because of natural business growth.

Beyond retirements and economic expansion, other factors contribute to the shortage of a skilled workforce, including loss of embedded knowledge by the movement of experienced workers, a negative image of the manufacturing industry among younger generations, lack of STEM (science, technology, engineering and mathematics) skills among workers, and a gradual decline of technical education programs in public high schools.

With CEOs and manufacturing executives around the world identifying "talent-driven innovation" as the number one determinant of competitiveness, it stands to reason the implications of such a shortage are significant and can have a material impact on manufacturers' growth and profitability. For example, 82 percent of executives responding to the Deloitte Skills Gap Survey (Giffi, 2015) indicated they believe the skills gap will impact their ability to meet customer demands, and 78 percent believe it will impact their ability to implement new technologies and increase productivity. Executives also indicated the skills gap impacts the ability to provide effective customer service (69 percent), the ability to innovate and develop new products (62 percent), and the ability to expand internationally (48 percent).

Eighty percent of manufacturing executives reported they are willing to pay more than the market rates in workforce areas reeling under the talent crisis. Still, 60 percent of positions remain unfilled because of the talent shortage. This clearly indicates there are not a sufficient number of workers interested in manufacturing to fill these positions. On the front end, executives reported it takes an average of 94 days to recruit employees in the engineer/researcher/scientist fields, and an average of 70 days to recruit skilled production workers. Facing those numbers, it is no surprise why manufacturers report the most significant business impact of the talent shortage is their ability to meet customer demand.

Adding to manufacturers' challenges to fill jobs is the issue of overcoming industry perception. The Public Perception of Manufacturing Study conducted over the past six years by The Manufacturing Institute (2010-2016) and Deloitte (2015), consistently revealed that while Americans consider manufacturing among one of the most important domestic industries for maintaining a strong national economy, they rank it low as a career choice for themselves. Moreover, only 37 percent of respondents in the 2015 study indicated they would encourage their children to pursue a manufacturing career.

Interestingly, Americans with high industry familiarity in manufacturing tend to have more favorable perceptions, and they are twice as likely as those with no familiarity to encourage their children to pursue a manufacturing career. Thus, manufacturers need to examine not only how they promote, recruit and engage a younger workforce, but examine whether they truly *fit* the perceived stereotype. No matter how well planned, pursued, or proclaimed, no promotional program will ever be able to overcome the realities of an outdated organizational and industry culture.

CHAPTER TWELVE
The Fear of Tomorrow - The New "Toyota Way"

"Starting an evolution over revolution."

The way forward for mid-market manufacturers begins with a reality check. The reality check is not meant to be a revolution, but an evolution. The evolution begins with manufacturing organizations examining the way the business operates in regards to the challenges of growth, recruitment, and shrinking margins, Liker & Meier

(2006) developed a *Toyota Way Field Manual* to update the original Toyota Way. The field manual addresses the ever-changing environment created through digitization. Yet there is a need for a new field manual – a four-step process - for addressing the evolution of manufacturing's front-of-the-house operations.

Step #1 - Examine the Culture

If Kotter (1990/1995) is correct, and leadership is about coping with change, then leadership and change begins from the top down. Although there are likely many strong influencers throughout your organization, culture will only change when your leadership team changes expectations and behaviors. This begins with examining the current state. Has your organization been complacent for many years, even decades, only serving a handful of customers? If so, this is your immediate and largest risk, and first priority to address. If your organization operates with antiquated and outdated platforms and processes to support your customers, this is your second greatest risk and priority for change. To change culture, you must change expectations and how the organization reacts to the external environment. If the expectation is to only sustain the current state of affairs, change will never occur, and the current culture will remain deeply and comfortably entrenched.

As a leader, influencing culture change goes beyond the HR department, a *team building exercise*, or some other canned effort that employees will dismiss as a superficial act, and simply a gesture to keep the team comfortable, complacent, and compliant. You must make decisive changes and take clear actions that pave the way on how the current state will influence and move to the future state, and how that change needs to occur. Building consensus on change requires participation and involvement from key stakeholders within your organization: Shift managers, department heads, crew chiefs, and sales leaders – they all have a role to play. The active engagement of those leaders, including gathering input and feedback on the company's future direction, will help them better embrace the changes, and articulate them effectively to their teams and subordinates.   In effect, CEOs and executives must create a MAYA Mantra within the organization.

How Change Takes Place. It takes 21 days of consistent behavior to break a habit. Organizational culture change takes even more time. Unlike the business hierarchy of days past, where individuals blindly followed orders of their superiors, today's younger generation have many more options, and are actively jumping ship if they feel short-changed or marginalized. Other factors that may impact change efforts include if your organization has had multiple *cultural restarts* in the past. If so, individuals will gravitate towards the assumption that this "change" is more of the same. Like breaking a bad habit, consistency, transparency, and open communications from all areas of leadership on progress, are required to maintain lasting success.

Success, the Ford Way. A recent interview (Lorsch, 2016) with Alan Mulally, CEO of Ford, discussed the challenges when he took the helm in 2006. Ford was on the verge of bankruptcy, and had lost over 25 percent of its market share since 1990. With the company months away from running out of cash, the challenge he faced wasn't just financial; he had to get the management team working more collaboratively. The Ford culture was notorious for being cutthroat and competitive. The organization functioned more like individual companies, rather than a single entity, with information hidden from different functions rather than shared.

Starting with a series of regular meetings, Mulally gathered up leaders of all levels in the organization to share their updates and input. Using a color-coded system, (green for good, yellow for caution, and red for trouble), he found in the first several meetings; all charts were "green". Leaders were worried their colleagues would attack if they showed vulnerability. Over time, Mulally encouraged and built transparency, allowing the organization to more effectively work together and find solutions collaboratively. This type of *cultural leadership* is essential to help move an organization away from the status quo, effectively address core organizational issues, and consider the goals and risk for the organization.

Step #2 – Examine Opportunities, Goals and Risks

If you are complacent with your existing business growth and structure, your organization will be as well. A business' long term health and success depends on having an honest understanding of where your organization is headed, including opportunities, goals and risks. Within mid-market manufacturing, many companies are beholden to a handful of major customers who provide a steady cash flow. Often, there is little incentive or desire to expand business outside of these relationships, as sourcing new customers can be time consuming and costly. The downside is that old customers will often begin to generate new demands and pressures upon the supplier, and have absolute power to demand new requirements at anytime. These customers can also require full transparency of your business and production operations, enabling them to easily terminate that relationship at anytime if another supplier is more willing to concede to their requests.

Beholden to a handful of customers for the majority of your revenue stream has numerous downsides and risks. Organizations that are tied to a single industry are deeply impacted by economic downswings and cyclical changes, such as in the oil and gas sector, agriculture, or construction (Gilmer, 2015). If your business goal is to simply keep the lights on and coast on a *great relationship* with a few major customers, you must ask yourself the tough question: Do your customers feel the same way about you? If not, it is only a matter of time before that structure crumbles. We have all experienced the impact of economic declines, most recently in 2008. While there are cases when changes are unforeseen, your field sales force often has insights early on to customer pullback and industry unrest.

Yet, if you have a diverse and balanced client portfolio, those economic and industrial shifts will have a lesser impact, and risks on your overall organizational health.

Reducing Risk. Reducing organizational risk requires examining opportunities both inside and outside of the traditional sphere. Implementing strategies to make headway into new industries and applications is often the lowest hanging fruit. Examining new ways your operations, services, and products may be utilized outside of the current channels can not only generate new revenue, but also differentiate your company from competitors and maximize production capacity. This can impact every facet of the organization - from serving as production overflow for another supplier, to making products for other companies based on provided specs (utilizing your existing equipment, unused capacity, and skillsets). The bottom line is to identify how and where you want to grow, and establish goals along the way. The goals must pass the FAS-R Test: Are the goals Feasible, Acceptable, Sustainable, and if so, what are the Risks? (Shambach, 2004). The FAS-R Test does not just include people, processes, and production, but also infrastructure.

Step #3 – Examine the Infrastructure

When you examine goals and risk, one of the main impediments can be your existing infrastructure. Infrastructure may include the actual skillsets and training of your employees, data management, systems, and processes responsible for day-to-day operations. If you are limited to highly manual processes, proprietary to your operation, running on a non-scalable and antiquated platform, your opportunity to grow is restricted. For example, if there is no capacity for your existing sales and manufacturing systems to add a unique product and process into the mix easily and efficiently, diversifying your production portfolio will be not only costly, but time consuming and riddled with flaws.

Not having agile processes and platforms also hamper your ability to identify real risks within the organization. Do you have complete transparency to true, fully burdened costs across every operation in your organization? There is often an inordinate amount of what is considered *sunk costs*: those costs for things that you simply have to invest in because it's the "cost of doing business". Yet, as companies grow, these sunk costs will exponentially increase if the organization is operating within an old structure. It is essential to examine, using real data analysis, time studies, and process mapping, to clearly understand where money is being spent and invested effectively, and where it is being wasted. This is where the application of technology comes in.

Often as revenues decline, the first action taken is to focus on increasing sales. While the decline may be because of the loss of a key customer or economical factors, there is consistently an underlying slow bleed of incrementally increasing costs of running the business. Many times, manufacturers will often reexamine raw materials suppliers, tightening up costs along with reducing excess headcount as orders shrink. These measures are beneficial, but often only temporary solutions to a long-term issue. Looking at your operations comprehensively and examining individual department processes, provides a more balanced view of how to effectively reduce sunk costs long term.

For example, if one employee requires 10 steps to complete a task, and can only complete 5 tasks a day, reducing the amount of steps in half doubles their productivity. Moving a traditionally paper-based process to digital eliminates not only the cost of paper, but also all associated components including extra printers, maintenance costs, and office supplies, not to mention the "fire drill" of finding that documentation when a key employee is out of the office (Burrows, 2012). Taking your business processes at face value ensures you not only miss out on the short term benefits of reducing costs and increasing revenue, but the long term ability to capitalize on new opportunities as they present themselves.

Step #4 – Examine Communications

Once you have addressed your organization's culture, goals, risks, and infrastructure, the last yet most important element is communications. When we talk about communications, we are not speaking about just your employees. Communications spans across your organization, inside and outside. When examining your communications processes, it is essential to determine areas of ineffectiveness – places where miscommunication consistently occurs. This may be as simple as lack of follow-ups with customers, or uncoordinated shipping communications, to loss of opportunities for the sale of wear parts. Each of these miscommunications may occur because of either a lack of effective messaging, or a lack of intelligent automation (i.e. digital technology).

Ineffective communication comes in many forms. Most often, people recognize it within a failed marketing campaign that has little response or return. Ineffective communication can also manifest within other key departments, such as technical support, customer service, logistics, and sales.

Consider a situation where a customer service person shares outdated technical information with a caller, or when a service technician doesn't have a clear understanding of a customer issue until they get out to the field. We know all issues cannot be prevented, but examine how the information and data you have about your products, customers and technical issues is stored and accessed. Do employees have to make phone calls or emails to the *in-house expert* or can they access information on the question independently? Do your employees have to wade through hundreds of outdated documents to find the *latest version* that has the newest information, or can they look up specifications within a central system? Is information from field technicians centrally captured in a platform where customer service and manufacturing can see and identify areas where processes can be changed to eliminate a recurring problem?

Marketing, or Marketing Communications (MARCOM) is traditionally seen as a customer-facing function, where communications are centered on promoting the company and its products. Yet communications goes beyond that traditional, externally facing view of marketing's role. Marketing can and should lead the way to optimize organizational communications.

If marketers are charged with managing external communications, then they should be responsible for internal processes as well. This includes identifying how information is structured, organized, and delivered throughout the company. Effective communications requires collaboration with multiple departments to identify bottlenecks. It requires an understanding and ability to work with the IT team to implement automation systems and data management platforms. It requires the ability to define and streamline a workflow, to reduce time spent, possibility for errors and increase capacity to scale up when needed. It requires the development of communications process strategies.

Many organizations view establishing effective communications as a daunting and costly task, but it does not have to be tackled all at once. Like eating an elephant, it should be taken one bite at a time. Determine the areas causing the most pain and cost, and take those on first. Identify areas that increase organizational risk, and define a plan to address and mitigate the risks. Over the course of time, not only will your organization transform, but these changes will also impact and support cultural change as a downstream effect.

CHAPTER THIRTEEN
When It's Too Late

"It will never happen here."

It is important to be completely honest about your business. Does your organization truly have its head in the sand when it comes to possible downfalls? Are you blissfully optimistic about growth and profits? Do you feel that if you simply keep pushing harder and faster, that it will all pay off in the end? If you keep doing what you've

131

always done, you will get what you have always gotten, *maybe*.

Mid-market manufacturers are notorious for holding onto the past. Those past successes, often stemming from events that occurred decades ago, lose their steam in the present. Many organizations have ignored the slow decline for so long, that once the final key customer has pulled back on orders or even parted ways with the organization, the entire operation is on the doomsday clock. When this occurs, it is often too late to recover. Those organizations, mired in their old ways, with a workforce that has not advanced their skillsets in years, has simply one of two choices. Sell or close.

Research has shown (Stalk, 2012) that by the third generation of ownership, over 90 percent of small to mid-sized businesses fail. Why is this the case? More often than not, the second and third generation owners grew up within the organization, right out of school, working for the business. Gaining experience in many capacities, from the shop floor to the front office, those owners lacked an outside perspective. Having never worked for another company, another industry, or often even in another town, their understanding of best business practices comes from what they saw and lived every day. It is virtually impossible to generate new ideas and implement change when you have not experienced any.

New ideas are typically hijacked from larger competitors, piggy-backed from what is perceived as *if they are doing it, it must be working*. Often times those organizations get caught in the Me-Too cycle: Simply replicating activities that they see within the sales, marketing and operations space of competitors, fueled by perspectives and opinions from the field sales team. Although this information may be all well and good, the critical element missing is the insight on *why* a competitor took a specific action. Did the competitor see a new market opportunity, or was the new product based on the whim of the owner? Do they have a true understanding of the marketplace or just had a key customer with a unique need that they felt would be cost-effective to promote more broadly? Are they really breaking new ground, or simply recycling old ideas?

More importantly, competitors' actions typically give no transparency to larger, more cost-impacting processes. Did they implement a new JIT manufacturing process? There is no way to really know. Did competitors implement a new ERP system, allowing them to process orders more efficiently and reduce overhead by 30 percent? Did the increase in efficiency in turn allow for a drop in their sale price? No way to really know. The back-story is critical to effectively evaluate a competitor's position in the market, whether a public or private company.

Creating a Commotion. If you are already 'behind the eight ball' and are bleeding cash, no 'silver-bullet' marketing campaign or magic software platform will effectively change your trajectory. You have to immediately begin to 'think outside of the box' on where you can generate revenue. Of course, costs come into play, but when you cut your operations down to the quick, you often can lose essential functions and employees from where you cannot truly recover. New revenue should come not only from low-hanging fruit, including past and current customers, but also creative channels, such as new industries, new applications, and new products altogether. Market analysis requires examining and identifying pain points in the market where you can fill a need. Bring your entire team together in a unified front to generate new ideas and approaches. Establish a plan and stick to it. The biggest opportunity for failure is running in too many directions at once.

From Commotion to Chaos. If you still believe everything's going to be fine if you simply wait it out, there may be a tough road ahead. As your organization declines, employee morale will follow, with key employees leaving for more stable opportunities. Those people remaining will become overworked in trying to cover the spread, and customer service, product quality, delivery times and overall performance will suffer. Customers will, in reaction, continue to turn to competitors and other suppliers they view as higher performing and more stable. Once you hit the point of no return, where you cannot deliver with your skeleton crew, it will be time to liquidate. While this seems like a dire prophecy, hundreds of manufacturing organizations face it daily (Newsweek Staff, 2010). You can continue to avoid the inevitable or you can take on the challenge. It's about owning your future or letting it be written for you. Sometimes a disruption is required to implement change.

CHAPTER FOURTEEN
The Way Forward

"It begins with collaboration."

No matter if you are at the beginning of your journey or have not even started, it is essential to first step out of your environment. When the pressure is on to meet quarterly targets and you are continually slipping behind, it is hard to justify a *time out*, but it is the most critical part of starting on the right track. Whether it is increasing your reading of business publications, attending a conference, joining a CEO advisory board, working with a coach or mentor, or hiring an outside consultant, you need to establish a genuine and comprehensive view of your business' current state and future challenges. The old adage of not being able to see the forest through the trees may not apply, because the trees have all fallen.

Leaders within an organization are often too close to the problems to define the root cause. Some leaders feel as though identifying a problem reflects poorly on them and their performance, which could not be further from the truth. An employee who does not stand up and voice concerns, provide insights on possible risks, or take initiative towards positive change, are the same individuals that are dragging down your organization and maintaining the status quo. As the leader, you set the bar of performance and expectations, and have to set the standard for the rest of the organization. This requires leading the efforts for organizational and cultural change.

While many small businesses are cash conscious, it can cost you little to no money to implement organizational change. Immediate opportunities often do not require a major investment in software, capital equipment, or a major advertising campaign, and provide a quick win that instills motivation in the organization. Many challenges are usually inherent to behaviors, attitudes and processes, which simply require discipline and oversight to change. The hardest part is determining which areas to address first, defining the changes needed, implementing those changes, and sustaining them over time. Remember the FAS-R Rule?

Identifying areas of change begins with creating a master list of challenge that span across departments, functions, internal and external to the organization. Suppliers, vendors, customers, employees, and everyone you engage with to operate the business. Your master list should be organized into a set of core areas in a grid-style format:

X-axis: Level of Importance

- Urgent/On Fire
- Address Later
- Examine Long Term

Y-axis: Type of Challenge

- Financial/Cost
- Customer Retention/Experience
- Employee Retention/Experience
- Competitive
- Product/Service
- Process/Operation

Once your master challenge list is established, create a set of cross-functional high performance teams (HPTs) to address the *urgent* challenges. HPTs should be clearly given expectations, timelines, deliverables, including but not limited to:

- Clear milestones with deadlines
- Expectations of creative, out-of-the-box ideas
- Resources and access to best practices, consultants and advisors
- Multiple recommendations and approaches to challenges, including needed resources, estimated costs and sustainability recommendations
- Active engagement from company leaders

Each HPT should come to the table with a variety of options, all which should be examined in regards to implementation resource requirements, short/long term costs and implementation time. Most importantly, HPTs should examine what types of 'disruptors' should be used to address the challenge. Typically, this requires more than a single solution, but a combination of approaches, such as leveraging technology, process modification, cultural change, and communications strategies simultaneously.

This comprehensive view provides an organization insight to core areas of change, rather than short-term supplier cost savings or margin increase actions. While this exercise can be a challenge with a HPT indoctrinated from inside your current operations, forcing them to look outside the organization will help them examine not only ideas to address immediate needs, but very often, their own challenges. This process is the beginning for starting a culture of continuous improvement, and continuing to learn and examining new and better ways to do things. It serves as the catalyst for change.

How this input from the HPT is addressed and handled both short term and long term is the second half of the equation. Gaining participation, engagement, and momentum to address change cannot stall once those concepts and suggestions are presented. More often than not, employees working within a status quo environment have voiced and recommended new ideas at least 10 times within their first year of work, but saw or noted no recognition or follow through from management on their ideas.

While not all ideas can be implemented or implemented immediately, it is important to ensure there is a clear feedback loop on ideas and recommendations. This should follow a three-tiered process:

- If the idea has immediate merit, communicate how they can be involved
- If the idea is a long-term merit, be clear on the timeline to readdressing it and follow-through
- If the idea is undetermined to have merit, identify how it will be assessed and in what timeframe

The key to success is follow-through. People value having their ideas listened to and being respected, no matter their position within the company. Success is not about implementing the most ideas, but selecting those with the highest level of impact, involving and empowering employees to implement that idea, and consistently engaging by listening and follow ups. These simple actions will not only provide a direction for immediate change, but also serve as a platform for a culture shift.

No company is without it's risks, challenges, and opportunities. Mid-sized manufacturers have an even steeper climb. The boom of the industrial era led to a mass amount of growth, only to see that transform through outsourcing, offshoring, technology, automation and a new generation of tech-savvy Millennials. These realities are not going away. Private suppliers will continue to feel the financial pinch, getting pressured by customer overlords to reduce overhead. Companies moving into second and third generation owners will be shuttered or sold off because of declining revenues. The future of manufacturing in the United States as it once was, is in the hands of today's small business owners.

There is an opportunity to change the future of how we view manufacturing - how it can be a career for future generations, rather than viewed as antiquated, dangerous and unstable.

Manufacturing has been the heart of our economy here in the Midwest, and across the nation. We want manufacturing to be alive and well for generations, but we first all have to see and agree that the time for change is now.

CHAPTER FIFTEEN
Temet Nosce – "Know Thyself"

Know thyself. It is a simple concept, yet elusive for many business owners. When an organization is under the gun to produce revenue and profits, the easiest action is to press harder on all sales fronts, take sweeping cost-cutting actions, and fulfill any customer request. In the short-term, targets might eventually be met, with a major downsizing staved off.

Long-term, those tactics are not sustainable. Continually running from fire-to-fire, living in reactionary mode, leaves little time for examining and implementing strategic growth. Though today's manufacturers often feel there is little time to consider the long-term, only thinking about the short-term is not simply a downward spiral, but a trap, where cash-strapped companies often cannot escape.

With steadfast determination and hard work - the essence of how manufacturing was founded - the industry can pull itself up from the depths of despair. The first step in this journey is for organizations to take a long, hard, honest look internally, and identify their true capabilities and opportunities. This requires a level of practical, logical, and strategic examination of the company as a whole, starting at the beginning.

Who We Are. Sometimes it is best to begin at the beginning. Where did the company start? What are our roots? The original founder often had simply a skillset and an idea. Over time, the company grew a <u>reputation</u>, whether for quality, a unique product, a low cost, or a combination thereof. This reputation became the *brand position* in the mind of customers (think John Deere = Tractors). Growth catapulted through the acquisition of smaller manufacturers, along with securing multi-year contracts with major, global customers. This revenue stream *fed the beast* for subsequent decades as the economy flourished, and business was good.

As manufacturers continued to churn out products, opportunities for product diversification came about, with line extensions and new industry penetration. Profits continued to pour in. Then, all of a sudden, an economic downturn occurs, offshoring begins, and regulations come into play, all of which begins to influence income. Those companies that had been simply cashing checks from a handful of key customers started to feel the impact. Without continued modernization of processes, technology, equipment, employee training, marketing, and strategy, companies were in a catch-up mode. Those without big coffers have scrambled ever since.

Failure seemed sudden, but the writing was on the wall.

Sudden Death Overtime. Often, the circumstances of the downward spiral were at least partially avoidable. Even without a crystal ball, manufacturers frequently lost sight of what made them great. Whether that was something tangible like product quality, or intangible, like an honest sales approach, as the organization grew, those qualities/attributes were lost. When marketing and promotions attempted to reinforce the message, the company could not fulfill the promises like in the past. Differentiation as a strength and opportunity began to decline, and commoditization as a weakness and a threat, began to set in.

Sales and production, driven and incentivized by units out the door, had a stronger influence in recent years on the operations of manufacturers. While these are critical functions, sales departments often don't examine or consider the long-view – how the company can further differentiate and serve in ways outside of the traditional transaction methods of simple product delivery. The company's founders often saw the bigger picture, yet when pressure for ever-growing profits drive the company, behavior inherently changes.

This means having a better understanding of the customer and their challenges from a business perspective. Companies do not just purchase products and services; they are looking to solve a problem. This can manifest itself in the simplest form, with buying a component rather than manufacturing it. Yet for organizations that truly understand their customers and their operations, it can be much, much, more.

The Customer Conundrum. Consider a customer that purchases a series of widgets from your company. They purchase from you because of the <u>quality</u> of your offering, along with your <u>fast turnaround time</u>, and <u>consistent delivery</u>. Additionally, the customer has other widgets they purchase from competing manufacturers. Are these widgets your company could produce? More importantly, could you offer a more efficient design and production process that provide them not only cost advantages, but also a component that helps <u>them</u> differentiate within their marketplace?

How about your business practices? Does it cost customers little time and effort to do business with you? Is the ordering and inventory process completely automated, so customers do not have to utilize internal resources to manage *you* as a supplier? Are you using smart systems to proactively inform customers of inventory shortages by component, so as not to disrupt their production processes? What about a series of tools, processes, and programs to effectively and efficiently train the customers' teams on how to troubleshoot your components if there is an issue in the field? Can customers troubleshoot remotely, to eliminate downtime? Manufacturers tend to only look at their businesses as a production facility, and not a customer-serving, problem-solving operation. These customer-oriented, forward-thinking concepts give a manufacturer a unique differentiation, which other widget makers cannot replicate. Addressing the customer conundrum is the essence of effective positioning and strategy.

The dream of the original founder likely was not to be the maker of the *most* components, but the maker of the <u>*best*</u> components. Quality often defined the "best", but more often than not, an intimate understanding of customer needs beyond the obvious. Small business owners saw an opportunity in the marketplace being inadequately addressed, and knew that designing and delivering a solution to the problem would create the success the company needed. Today's manufacturers have lost this fundamental understanding:

Know thyself and know thy customers.

The result? Reduced value and high commoditization. Without a better yardstick, no wonder customers are continuing to compare suppliers solely on price, without other benefits to measure. Smart manufacturers will embrace knowing thyself as an opportunity rather than a threat, to go from good to great, and create an eruption in growth, through a disruption of the status quo.

By examining and embracing change, potential 'disruptors' can become opportunities to differentiate and compete effectively in the long term. Whether new technologies, cultural change, expanded marketing investments, connecting with a younger workforce or all of the above, manufacturing can become the new industry of "Innovation in America".

About the Author

Andrea Belk Olson is a 4-time ADDY® award-winner and founder of Prag'madik, a marketing and communications strategic consulting firm. (www.pragmadik.com) With 20 years of direct, digital, social, technology and content marketing expertise, Ms. Olson helps industrial organizations exceed customer growth and cost-reduction expectations. She is Pragmatic Marketing and SCIP II Certified, with over 40 published works on marketing differentiation and best practices.

About Prag'madik

Prag'madik designs solutions to optimize front-of-the-house operations. Everything customer-facing, whether branding, marketing, strategy, technology platforms or processes. Think of us as "Lean for Marcom". We focus on areas of true impact: operational waste, opportunities for new revenue, and the elimination of inefficiencies. We don't sell generic solutions, we partner with you to resolve real business challenges.

Contact Prag'madik
Andrea Belk Olson, Founder / CEO
andrea.olson@pragmadik.com
www.pragmadik.com

Twitter: @pragmadik
Blog: www.pragmadik.com / #blog_news

REFERENCES

Baran, R. (2012, Feb). Business process automation: The hidden costs of paper. *Positive Vision*. Retrieved from http://www.positivevision.biz/blog/bid/122704/Business- Process-Automation-The-Hidden-Costs-of-Paper

Boeriu, H. (2009, July). How to: Follow a new BMW from order, to shipping, to delivery. *BMW Blog*. BMWBlog.com. Retrieved from http://www.bmwblog.com/2009/07/14/how-to-follow-a-new-bmw-from-order-to-shipping-and-to-delivery/

Boyer, K.K. & Moutray, C. (2013). Advanced manufacturing techniques. *The National Center for the Middle Market and the National Association of Manufacturers*. Retrieved from http:// www.middle marketcenter.org/Media/Documents/advanced-manufacturing-techniques-among-us-middle-market-manufacturers_ advanced_manufacturing_report.pdf

Burrows, M. (2012). Operational efficiency – It's not just about cost cutting. *BSMReview.com Business Service Management Review*. Retrieved from http://www.bsmreview.com/oppseff.shtml

Cameron, K. S. (1994, Summer). Successful strategies for organizational downsizing. *Human Resource Management*, 33(2), 189–211. doi: 10.1002/hrm.3930330204

Campbell-Dollaghan, K. (2013). Raymond Loewy, the man who made the 20th century beautiful. *Gizmodo*. Retrieved from http://gizmodo.com/ raymond -loewy-the-man-who-made-the-20th-century-beauti-1458724316

Carroll, L. (1865). *Alice in wonderland*. Alice-in-Wonderland.net. Retrieved from http://www.alice-in-wonderland.net/

Dam, R. F. (2016). The MAYA principle: Design for the future, but balance it with your user's present. *Interaction Design Foundation*. Retrieved from https://www. interaction-design.org/literature /article/design-for-the-future-but-balance-it-with-your-users-present

Davis, S. & Kay, D. (2004). Cutting costs: Should personnel be the first to go? *Employment Practices Solutions*. Retrieved from http://www.epspros.com/News Resources/Newsletters?find=14020

Driscoll, M. (2011). Cutting the costs of sales order processing. *Business Finance*. BusinessFinancemag.com. Retrieved from http://businessfinancemag.com/bpm/cutting-costs-sales-order-processing

Drucker, P. F. (1967/2006). *The effective executive.* New York, NY: HarperCollins Publishers

DTMD (2011). The struggle is real. *DTMD: Makin Dollas*. Retrieved from http://knowyourmeme.com/ memes/ the-struggle-is-real

Duke II, J. E. & Udono, E. N. (2012). A new paradigm in traditional human resource management practices. *Journal of Management and Sustainability*. Canadian Center of Science and Education. doi: http://dx.doi.org/10.5539/jms.v2n2p158

Gallatin, R. (2016). Raymond Loewy on the cover of Time magazine. *Avanti*. Retrieved from

http://www.theavanti.net/timemagazine.ht
ml

Giffi, C. et al. (2015). Skills gap in U.S.
manufacturing 2015 and beyond. *Deloitte
Manufacturing Institute*. Retrieved from
http://www.themanufacturing
institute.org/~/
media/827DBC76533942679A15
EF7067A704CD.ashx

Gilmer, R. W. (2015). Houston outlook grows
darker as the oil downturn becomes deeper
and longer. *Institute for Regional Forecasting*.
Bauer College of Business: University of
Houston. Retrieved from
http://www.bauer.uh.edu/centers/irf/hou
ston-updates-june15.php

Grunewald, M. (2014, March). Why more
employees are considering leaving their
companies. *LinkedIn*. Retrieved from
https://business. linkedin.com/ talent-
solutions/ blog/2014/03/internal-mobility-
exit-survey

Kotter, J. P. (1990/1995). What leaders really do. In
J. Thomas Wren (Ed.), *Leader's Companion:
Insights on leadership through the ages* (pp. 114-

123). New York: Free Press. (Reprinted from *Harvard Business Review*, (1990).)

Liker, J. K. (2004). *The Toyota way*. New York: NY. McGraw-Hill

Liker, J. K. & Meier, D. (2006). *The Toyota way: The field companion*. New York: NY. McGraw-Hill.

Lorsch, J. W. & McTague, E. (2016. April). Culture is not the culprit. *Harvard Business Review*. Retrieved from https://hbr.org/2016/04/culture-is-not-the-culprit

McCutcheon, B. (2012). A homecoming for US manufacturing. *PriceWaterhouseCoopers*. Retrieved from http://www.pwc.com/us/en/ industrial-products/publications/us-manufacturing-resurgence.html

Nager, A. B., & Atkinson, R. D. (2015). The myth of America's manufacturing renaissance: The real state of U.S. manufacturing. *ITIF -The Information Technology and Innovation Foundation*. Retrieved from http://www2.itif.org /2015-myth-american-manufacturing-renaissance.pdf?_

ga=1.54615979.1631991617.1468031677

Nanney, R., Michaels, H., Goverman, I., & Rosone, B. (2014). Technology in the Mid-Market: Perspectives and priorities. *Deloitte.* Retrieved from http://www2. deloitte. com/content /dam/Deloitte/lu/Documents/ manufacturing/us_dges_Deloitte_TechSurve y2014.pdf

Nanney, R. et al. (2015). Disruption in the mid-market: How technology is fueling growth. *Deloitte.* Retrieved from http://www2.deloitte.com/content/dam/ Deloitte/us/Documents/Deloitte%20Growt h%20Enterprises/us-dges-deloitte-report-disruptionin-mid-market.pdf

Newsweek Staff. (2010). The case against layoffs: They often backfire. *Newsweek Business.* Retrieved from http://www.newsweek .com/case-against-layoffs-they-often-backfire-75039

O'Connell, C. (2014). Why agencies need acquisition as-a-service. *InformationWeek Government.* Retrieved from http://www. informationweek.com/

government/cloudcomputing/why-agencies-need-acquisition-as-a-service/a/d-id/ 1269500? page_number=2

Prest, G. (2015). Traditional supply chain models will be extinct in 2025, thanks to these disruptors. *Inbound Logistics.* Thomas Publishing Company. Retrieved from http://www.inbound logistics .com/cms/article/traditional-supply-chain-models-will-be-extinct-in-2025-thanks-to-these-10-disruptors/

Rakowski, L. (2003). Moving to Lean Manufacturing. *Modern Machine Shop.* Retrieved from http://www. mmsonline.com/articles/ moving-to-lean-manufacturing

Shambach, S. A. (2004). *Strategic Leadership Premier* (2Ed). Department of Command, Leadership and Management. Carlisle Barracks, PA: United States Army War College

Sheth, A. (2015). Disrupt or be disrupted. *Sales for Life*. Retrieved from http://www.salesforlife.com/blog/sales-management/disrupt-or-be-disrupted-40-of-companies-will-be-extinct-in-10-years/

Stalk, G. & Foley, H. (2012). Avoid the traps that can destroy family businesses. *Harvard Business Review*. Retrieved from https://hbr.org/2012/01/avoid-the-traps-that-can-destroy-family-businesse

Taylor, T. (2016). The Cost of Training New Employees, Including Hidden Expenses. ADP. Retrieved from http://www.adp.com/thrive/articles/the-costs-of-training-new-employees-including-hidden-expenses-3-157

Thackray, A., Brock, D., & Jones, R. (2015). *The Life of Gordon Moore, Silicon Valley's Quite Revolutionary*. Retrieved from https://en.wikipedia.org/wiki/Moore%27s_law

66488649R00105

Made in the USA
Charleston, SC
20 January 2017